Meeta Nihalani, Ashish Mathur

Education Quality Impacts the Employment Generation

GRIN Verlag

Bibliografische Information der Deutschen Nationalbibliothek:

Die Deutsche Bibliothek verzeichnet diese Publikation in der Deutschen National-
bibliografie; detaillierte bibliografische Daten sind im Internet über http://dnb.d-
nb.de/ abrufbar.

Imprint:

Copyright © 2011 GRIN Verlag GmbH
Druck und Bindung: Books on Demand GmbH, Norderstedt Germany
ISBN: 978-3-656-09336-7

This book at GRIN:

http://www.grin.com/en/e-book/184475/education-quality-impacts-the-employment-
generation

GRIN - Your knowledge has value

Der GRIN Verlag publiziert seit 1998 wissenschaftliche Arbeiten von Studenten, Hochschullehrern und anderen Akademikern als eBook und gedrucktes Buch. Die Verlagswebsite www.grin.com ist die ideale Plattform zur Veröffentlichung von Hausarbeiten, Abschlussarbeiten, wissenschaftlichen Aufsätzen, Dissertationen und Fachbüchern.

Visit us on the internet:

http://www.grin.com/

http://www.facebook.com/grincom

http://www.twitter.com/grin_com

Education Quality Impacts the Employment Generation

Dr. Meeta Nihalani
Head, Department of Management Studies
Jai Narain Vyas University Jodhpur

Dr. Ashish Mathur
Associate Professor, Department of Management Studies
Lachoo Memorial College of Science and Technology, Jodhpur

Abstract

The power of human excellence lies on applying human intention to explore potential connections so as to create interactions with more valuable knowledge to build the academic wealth of the country. The education is the soft wealth of any country because it develops the intellectual capital of the economy to foster the development and growth of the economy. The government can only make people prosperous by giving them the right education to cultivate the skills and competencies to design their destinies and employment to live a dignified lie. The employment potential of the economy can be increased but converting the masses into the trained human resources to develop the options and opportunities to harness the resources to foster the growth and development of the country. The aim of the papers is to design the strategic framework for developing the education to cultivate the right the right competencies to grow in an empowered way

Key words- development, quality, education, student satisfaction, employment

Introduction

The impact of the global economy has given the huge options of jobs and opportunities to the people to satisfy the vast demand of the people in the global markets. The people can respond to the global employment options, if they have the quality education and the competency to connect in an easy way to give solutions to the business and markets. The aim of education should relate to the development of enterprises and giving them the practices and ethics to grow in a sustainable way. The economy is growing with specialization and knowledge. The impact of technology and the connectivity is requiring more talented pool of people who can connect and collaborate to the international needs of the market. The business has become complex with the impact of various socio- cultural forces. The understanding requires the study of the marketing in terms of social and economic parameters to design the products according to the global needs. The global era is becoming more demanding because of the latest development of research to respond to the changing needs of the consumers.

The impact of education on human life can generate employment by:
- Building professional competencies
- Building the computer skills
- Building the talent
- Building the confidence
- Building the communication

The value of quality education for creating employment

Any economy of the country has the potential for the skilled, unskilled and semi-skilled employment options available. The trainers and mentors need to understand the background and the interest of the students to cultivate the right skills, so as to match with market demand. The institutes require the collaboration of the industry to build the understanding of the needs of the society and developing the talents of students to connect to the local hubs of building business in sustainable way. The quality of education can enhance the employment if the education focuses on the following issuers:
- Developing the methods to of university of learning and the strategies developed for achieving a responsive university.
- Focusing on research and students are participants
- Focusing on learning and growing

- Fostering continuous improvement
- Building collaborative models
- Building the academic productivity
- Building the organizational performance
- Fostering the radical changes through technology
- Building the empirical education and research
- Supporting self-analysis and self-awareness
- Fostering quality improvement
- Focusing on strategic development
- Focusing on teaching and counseling
- Building mentors and coachers
- Developing and training the faculty
- Building the diversified ND specified course
- Be loping the material and resource
- Building the concepts and clarity
- Focusing on the specific industry needs
- Designing specific course to build the specialization
- Focusing on developing and building workshops

Literature review

According to Grant (2002, 2004) Widrick (2002) - The quality of higher education relates to following dimensions

- quality of design
- conformance and performance

According to Borahan and Ziarati (2002) - The quality in education can be combined with total quality management tools to build quality assurance and control including

- programme management and operations
- curriculum design content and organization
- teaching, learning and assessment
- student support and guidance
- quality assurance and enhancement

According to Becket and Brookes, (2006) - the model of quality management has six dimensions

- internal/external perspective
- qualitative/quantitative information
- snapshot/longitudinal timespan
- quality dimension assessed
- system elements
- enhancement or assurance focus

According to Reid and Shelby (2002) – The tangible benefits from internal audits on quality control of education can give a significant cultural change which can reinforce quality enhancement to:

- create greater staff involvement
- give benefits to the institutions
- programme management
- development and evaluation
- staff development
- assessment of students
- external examining processes
- Collaborative provision.

The impact of environment on quality education

The educational institute's works in a system which is exposed to the external forces of change in form of technological, socio-cultural and technological forces. The legal political environment also influences the colleges and the higher educational institutes because of the changing values. The educational institutes need to work with faculty and experts to work in a coordinated way to get the benefits of the latest materials and research coming into the market. The relations with industry can build the placement potential for the institutes.

Figure – 1 the environmental impact on the educational institutes

The quality of education delivered by the institutes is impacted by the following factors:

- Investment and finances
- Industry needs
- Professionalism of business organizations
- Structured approach for teaching
- Price and affordability
- Volume of research
- Involvement of students

The resources at of education should available at reasonable prices. The cost of education is influenced by attention to the following areas.

- Focus on process of change management
- Focus on demand of the market and designing of courses according to them
- Focus on value chain configuration to connect to sources of data and information
- Knowledge development and sharing.

The technical improvement in the developing the education process can build the better communication systems with the faculties and the experts to build the specifications which can be created with the technical emphasis on value analysis. The innovation analysis and the creativity can put the impact on the quality of education development. The change process engineering can build the optimum cost for the knowledge development. The change management process can improve the design and development of the syllabus.

The quality education builds the empowered teams for the business organizations

The educational institutes should focus on quality learning toehnace the skills and foster

- teamwork and composition and top management support
- Education and Business plan and vision
- Effective communication
- Project management
- Appropriate business and legacy system
- Software development
- Testing and troubleshooting
- Effective – decision making
- Effective training

Building quality standards

The quality ethics are important for the educational institutes and they relate to:

- Identification of the students need and their feedback
- Emphasis on the quality learning and improvement
- Exploring a range of analytical tools and techniques for problem solving developing the competencies

- Empowering the faculty for improving quality in building the knowledge practices.

The students need

The students the basis of the economic development of any country and they need
- value for money invested
- education that provides employment
- delivery with quality and up gradation
- Quality faculty and student interface.

The strategic orientation to build the efficient educational system for the institute's strategic orientation for the firm needs to focus on the resource utilization by maintaining the sustainability of the system. The right combination with waste minimization is important to enhance the performance. This requires the designing of the enablers to catalyze the development to gain the competitive edge in the markets. The enablers could be efficient and talented teams to harness the potential of market. The better designing of the improvement systems also enables cost reduction to enhance the profitability. Therefore the operational excellence can be achieved by
- Strategy
- Performance to improve the cost structures
- Enablers- resource development to give the better products to the society

The designing of the successful business models

The successful educational institutes can investment in designing the knowledge products in such a way that they meet the market demand. The courses and programmes can have the competitive edge by empowering the students. The focus has to be on:
- Manage faculty and integrate with the industry experts
- Build the education quality assessment system
- Basic tools student communication
- Focus on academic performance and build the personnel and capital
- Build the knowledge link with the technology integration
- Integrating education and values by providing the counselors

Conclusion

The quality is important for the educational institutes to generate the employment for the economy. The educational institutes need to focus on the problem-solving skills and build the teams with leadership skills to manage the group learning process. The improvement and control tools and techniques can foster better learning practices. The understanding of the students can impart better training to them. The student care is important by giving them the healthy environment for learning and responding.

References

1. Borahan, N. G. and Ziarati, R. (2002) Developing Quality Criteria for Application in the Higher Education Sector in Turkey. Total Quality Management, 13(7), 913-926. doi:10.1080/0954412022000017021
2. Grant, D., Mergen, E. and Widrick, S. (2002) Quality Management in US Higher Education. Total
3. Quality Management, 13(2), 207-215. doi:10.1080/09544120120102441
4. Grant, D., Mergen, E. and Widrick, S. (2004) A Comparative Analysis of Quality Management in US and International Universities. Total Quality Management, 15(4), 423-438.
5. Becket, N. and Brookes, M. (2006) Evaluating Quality Management in University Departments. Quality Assurance in Education, 14(2), 123-142. doi:10.1108/09684880610662015
6. Reid, K. and Ashelby, D. (2002) The Swansea Internal Quality Audit Processes: a case study. Quality Assurance in Education, 10(4), 237-245. doi:10.1108/09684880210446910